B&T LUMINARY
GROUP

Complete Guideline
To Run a Rental Car
Company on Turo

By

Willy Tchango

Table of Contents

About the Authors

Willy Tchango, of Cameroonian origin, is an international student in the United States. Tchango is finding his way in the world of business, truly seeking the "American Dream". Louise Bissek, Tchango's fiancée, was herself an entrepreneur running an electronic business prior to joining her expertise and know-how to Willy's. Following years of deliberation and discussions, the pair decided to work together on a common goal: launching their rental car business. Joining their forces together, Willy and Louise have been running the B&T Luminary Group LLC since July 2021 and have seen tremendous success. Starting with only one car, the BMW X1, they have now expanded their float to over 30 cars within one year. They furthermore have completed over 1000 trips as this book is being written.

In this eBook, they present their experience and what they have learned throughout the process, namely helping *you* start your very own business. From sharing how they learned about putting processes in place to build business credit, to explaining how they acquired cars and reinvested their profits into scaling their business every month, this book teaches you all you need to know to succeed with a car rental business.

Summary

Has the following ever happened to you? Perhaps you see someone driving a different car every day or week, and you are not sure if they are rich or not. You might look at them in envy or wonder, *how do they do it*? The answer is simple: it is because they are renting them. Car-renting businesses are growing tremendously, and they are gaining an immense market share as we speak. Individuals like you and me are willing to rent cars for cheap by the day, hour, or week. As a result, the business model is profitable and has a lot of competition. Additionally, the freedom to move around, the comfort aspect, as well as the ease of use and low price all work to increase the business' attractiveness. Not only this, but individuals who cannot afford to buy a car now can rent one if they need to, without needing to go in debt or without needing to purchase low-quality cars that may only last a few months. It is estimated that by 2029, the industry will be worth $141.17 billion, while it currently stands at $98 billion as this book is being written. So, what has pushed this growth, you wonder? There are a few reasons, but a key one is that it is getting more expensive to own a car or to use taxi services/car-sharing services such as Uber and Lyft. In fact, the rules and policies the government has put in place have greatly affected these taxi companies. However, there is hope: the cost-effective leasing model that was just set up will help rental car businesses grow in the future.

Starting a rental car business in Texas is difficult, but with proper business planning, you can start from scratch and make significant profits. That being said, although this business model is profitable and competitive, it is fraught with danger. Giving someone the keys to one's car, trusting that they will use it properly while one is away, and that they will return it in good condition is a risk that one must take. People hire cars for work or pleasure, and due to the high demand for taxi services and the current limited supply, Texas is an ideal location for establishing a business in this sector.

While the supply is limited, this sector is nonetheless quite competitive. Therefore, effective marketing methods are required. However, it is vital to remember that the state authorities have established numerous laws, guidelines, and restrictions for entrepreneurs who wish to create automobile rental enterprises in the state. The first step in acquiring a business license is obtaining a motor vehicle rental tax authorization. To rent a motor vehicle in Texas, such as a cab or trailer, a Texas Motor Vehicle Rental Tax Permit is required. The license stipulates all operating requirements for the business inside the market or state. With the increasing demand for rental automobiles in the United States, this e-book will show you how to create and operate a successful rental car business in Texas. The eBook also includes guidance for launching and managing a fleet on peer-to-peer platforms such as Turo – one of the most rapidly expanding internet platforms that connect automobile owners with clients.

Are you ready to learn? Let's get started.

Chapter One: The Basics of Starting a Rental Car Business

Many people believe running a rental car business is only for the wealthy. Today, you can start your own rental car business with just a few cars, or even your own car, if you are passionate about starting a business and making more money. To dispel doubts, remember that others have started businesses from scratch and are now multi-millionaires. So why should you not be able to do the same? Positivity and self-assurance are qualities that all entrepreneurs should possess.

First, to provide an overview of the business model, owning or operating a car rental company entails renting vehicles to consumers for a set amount of time at a reasonable price. The client pays based on the time they have used the car, while the owner, in most situations, gains based on the number of trips or the time taken (mileage, time of use, etc.). Consequently, it would be beneficial if you calculated the fees or payment rates based on the number of trips taken and the length of time the car was not in your possession. Other factors impact fees or rates of employment. Among these factors are the function and type of vehicles. The cost of repairs and risk reduction varies based on the make and model of the automobile.

Fortunately, platforms like Turo offer protection policies that define the amount of money you would be responsible for in the event of damage. To provide an example of how my wife and I began our business, in 2021, we started renting out our single personal vehicle on Turo. We began by renting a 2017 BMW X1 for $95 per day. We favored renting to business clients and small groups of vacationers in Texas. After some time, we expanded our fleet to include the Hyundai Tucson 2020, the Toyota C-HR 2018, the Volkswagen Jetta 2013, the Chevrolet Tahoe 2016, the Land Rover Range Rover Sport 2018, and the Volkswagen Passat 2017. Our experience with Turo gave us the tools to diversify our company's target market. Currently, our fleet on Turo consists of twenty-two rental vehicles, and our company intends to increase this number.

Getting Started

Running a Successful Fleet on Turo: How Does it Work?

Turo is the best place to start a car rental business because it is reputable and has a wide panoply of customers and car owners alike. The company has grown significantly over the last few years, and that growth is expected to continue as more individuals see the savings, they can make by renting a car as opposed to using car-sharing services. Turo is a great place to start a business renting out cars because a single listing can bring in up to $706 per month. The platform is also useful for people who own cars but cannot afford to pay for gas, maintenance, and monthly payments. That being said, a person must meet several requirements before they can perform any transaction on the platform.

The first step is to sign up for an account on the Turo website. Other factors, including whether or not the vehicles listed on the platform are eligible and whether or not they are in the same area, also affect how efficiently the registration process works. Individuals in the United States do not have to worry about whether or not they live in the same place.

Additionally, you must register cars under your name to list them on Turo. Otherwise, the legal owner must give you permission if you want to sign up under a different name. The vehicle should be in good shape and meet all of the rules outlined by Turo.

Once started, download the app to make the process of managing your business easier. With the app, you can keep track of trips and send your clients messages when necessary. Using the app, you can also send photos.

Orientation

Once the listing is created, tune the app settings to suit the business's goals, schedules, and desired earnings. Share your cars in your fleet to publicize the business and earn more opportunities. Sharing on other online platforms will earn you clients during your initial stage. With sharing, you can earn adequate cash that can enable you to offset other costs associated with owning a car, such as maintenance fees, fuel, and monthly payments. The company allows users to choose the protection plan best suits their business. This happens after pre-screening. All host protection plans in the United States come standard with $750,000 in third-party liability insurance issued to Turo under a policy from travelers, as well as varying levels of contractual reimbursement from Turo for physical damage and theft — the level of protection varies with the plan you choose.

Having a Hospitality Mindset

When hosting on Turo, you should always remember that you have entered a different form of the hospitality industry where neatness, cleanliness and high-quality customer care services are key for success. You are expected to be kind, flexible, and support others when you are able to do so. As an entrepreneur, you should focus on providing services and products that create a five-star experience for the clients. A remarkable aspect of the platform is that it rewards individuals and companies that work hard to provide five-star experiences to customers. For example, a fleet called All-Star Hosts has been awarded boosted booking opportunities, travel credit bonuses, priority support, and visibility in search results for providing high-quality services that meet customers' needs.

Build a Strong Foundation: Profile Polishing

They say a journey of a thousand miles begins with a single step. For a rental car business, the journey's beginning will determine the progress. Thus, begin polishing up the listing and your profile to make it pop. Listings that are polished thoroughly will rank higher during a search, attracting more guests into the fleets. Customers prefer more active fleets.

Uploading Photos

Uploading clear photos is another significant step when polishing the profile. It is recommended that you upload at least seven clear photos of the interior and exterior of the cars. The photos should be clear and well-lit. To achieve this, choose a nice background to take aspirations shots that stand out from the competitors. Hire a professional photographer if you do not have a clear camera or the necessary skills.

Describing the Cars

Provide a comprehensive list of the basic details of your cars on the platform. Structured options are used to provide these basic car details. The details may include fuel type, number of seats, and other unique features about the car. The unique features may include a four/all-wheel drive and a sunroof. Creativity is key when providing these listings. Also, you can include other features that make the listing more discoverable by guests. A unique description of the car should be shared as a form of a little personality, which can help a business go a long way! The guests should be provided with writing that informs them about the fun local drives, cleaning routines, and other interesting facts that can make them more excited and interested in booking the car. However, it would be best if you only used a small paragraph to provide these details since long descriptions can be too heavy to read for the guests.

Optimizing Settings

You should be familiar with the fleet's control center, the Host Hub. The Host Hub allows you to perform many actions, such as monitoring the performance metrics and adjusting the vehicle settings. It also facilitates the review of ratings and client reviews while tracking the earnings. Also, it allows for the account update on different level settings.

Update and Optimization of Availability

Another important setting is the update and optimization of availability. The availability calendar should always be updated since it informs new and regular guests of your availability. It is essential to block off all the cars that will not be available for trips to obtain trips that only work for the business' schedule. The availability calendar should be up to date to keep the performance metrics and avoid any trip cancellation. The tips to help you maximize your earnings include availing all cars on weekends, planning ahead of peak seasons, and keeping an eye out for long weekends and holidays. Weekends bear a large percentage of the total trips made during the week. Most trips begin on Friday or Saturday, making weekends twice as busy as the weekdays. Also, there is a high demand for cars for hire during the summer and fall holidays. Finally, keeping an eye out for long weekends is necessary since most guests plan last-minute gateways. They can be over three four-day weekends. Customizing the trip preferences will help the business get trips that best work for the company's shared goals and prices.

Book instantly is another way to get trips that are good for the business. With this feature, a guest can book a car without waiting for the owner to approve each trip manually. Even though the feature is turned on by default for new listings, it is best to keep it in sync with the calendar at all times. When the feature is turned on, the search ranking of the listing goes up. You should turn off the feature, though, if you need enough time to prepare for a trip so that you do not have to cancel it. By changing the settings for advance notice, you can decide how much time you need before each trip. It can be altered to fit any of the locations. For example, if a client likes to plan trips at the last minute, many trips will be blocked less than 48 hours before they start. So, lowering the number of days in advance will make it more likely that journeys will be booked at the last minute.

Furthermore, setting the trip-duration parameters will help you get the trips that work best for you. You should set the shortest and the longest-duration trips that you accept. You should try to allow shorter trips if it's possible. More than half of trips are two days or less, so you can book more if you prioritize shorter trips. Reviewing the distance limits by setting how far a client can travel by car daily is another factor that will attract clients that best suit the business. However, you should allow at least 250 miles per day to be strong in search rankings. You can even offer more to add a competitive advantage. Remember that although people do not like limits and boundaries, they often don't go as far as the boundaries and limits allow.

Additionally, pickup and return hours should be set, and availability should be indicated for check-in and checkout. To accommodate broader return and pickup hours, it is advisable to offer contactless check-ins and checkouts. Since clients prefer booking cars instantly, the calendar should honor the trips. Alternatively, Book Instantly should be turned off for a while if you need more time to prepare.

Pricing

Pricing the cars competitively is the easiest way to get more bookings. You can achieve proper pricing using Turo pricing tools that automatically price the cars. The tool uses an algorithm to optimize a car's daily price according to its demand patterns, seasonality, and local market. Alternatively, you can set the pricing manually by setting the daily rates. Manual pricing is achieved by monitoring the local demand patterns and using the information obtained to adjust prices accordingly. Conduct research on how other similar cars are priced around you and aim to price yours at a competitive or better price. You can adjust the prices if you do not achieve the expected traction. Most importantly, you should not overprice or underprice the cars.

Delivery and Extras

After establishing a solid base, publishing clear images, optimizing settings, and polishing the listings, consider bringing the listing to a new level by offering delivery and additional services. The listing would stand out more if it provided extraordinarily convenient deliveries to the guests. Delivery is an outstanding service that sets your firm apart from competitors and provides a market advantage. Fee-based delivery is available to railway stations, hotels, airports, and other destinations. You can add fees to each delivery to increase your earnings. Offering add-ons is an alternative method of earning each trip. Extras are optional add-ons that guests may purchase in conjunction with a vacation. A fantastic example would be the provision of picnic baskets, camping gear, or child safety seats. Similarly, you can enhance their Turo experience by providing post-trip cleaning and pre-paid fueling.

Generally, deliveries and extras not only make your services unique and outstanding, but they also give you an extra income on top of what you have earned from a trip. Many extras pay for themselves after a few days of short and long trips. The high-demand extras include post-trip cleaning, which costs $21 per trip, unlimited miles, which costs $59 per trip, and prepaid refueling, which costs $43 per trip. You should not give up if your car does not get booked after some time. Instead, you should try making the adjustments below:

➢ Enable Book Instantly.

➢ Price the car at the market rate or below.

➢ Add five more photos and more descriptions to your profile.

➢ Offer at least 200 miles/day.

Once a client has booked your car, you get a notification via email or the app. The next thing to do after receiving the notification is to countercheck the pre-trip checklist to ensure all bases are covered. Of course, no one would want to fail any procedure on your first trip. The procedure below should be followed using the checklist:

➢ Messaging the client to coordinate and agree on the pickup location and time.

➢ Cleaning the car properly and disinfecting it. You can use the guide on enhanced cleaning and disinfection.

➢ Recharge or refuel the car for the client to pick it up when it's got a full charge or tank.

➢ Take pre-tip photos that document the exterior and interior of the car, then upload them. The photos should be very clear. They should be uploaded on the "Trip photos" section for you to be legally eligible for the protection plan. It is important to note that Turo requires its hosts to provide pre and post pictures and other forms of evidence when processing a claim.

➢ Check in the guest with the Turo app at the beginning of the trip. Ensure that their driver's license is verified.

➤ See the guest off, then respond to concerns, messages, and extension requests. Otherwise, you can sit back and relax until it's checkout time!

➤ Receive payment after the client has returned the car. The payments are paid by direct deposit before three days elapse.

HINT: If you never want to miss any trip confirmation, you should use opt notifications by setting settings>Turo>Notifications.

Using a Turo Calculator to Estimate Earnings

Turo calculator is an easy-to-use tool that calculates the profits you can earn from renting a car on Turo. You need to select the car model you are renting and the location/area, and the calculator will automatically estimate the profits you will be earning per day. Luckily, Dallas is among the listed areas on Turo Calculator.

The calculator is reliable since it uses data from the market area to determine how much you can charge a client for your car. Also, an automatic pricing algorithm considers the demand for your car model in your market area or location. When using the calculator, it is essential to note that it assumes that you will be available throughout to complete all requests and that the car will be available for an average number of days. In addition, it believes that you chose the 70 plan where Turo will keep 30% of the daily costs to cater for operational expenses and other costs such as insurance coverage.

Although the Turo calculator is a fast, realizable, and easy-to-use method, some of its data might not be appropriate for your situation since the calculator produces results based on assumptions. In such a case, you can opt for a third-party Turo Calculator. This calculator allows you to personalize numerous data fields. You can also use it to customize information such as personal insurance costs, gas prices, and reimbursements from the government, among other personal details.

Illustration

BMW x1

The results above indicate that our average annual earnings for BMW X1 are $16,000. Finding Average Daily Earnings;

Average Daily Earnings=Average Annual Earnings/365

$$= 16,000/365= 48$$

The Average Daily Earning for renting a BMW X1 on Turo in Dallas is $48.

II. Hyundai Tucson 2020

The analysis above shows that the average annual earnings for a Hyundai Tucson are $14,800. Finding the Average Daily Annual Earnings;

Average Daily Earnings=Average Annual Earnings/365

$$=14,800/365= 40$$

The Average Daily Earning for renting a Hyundai Tucson on Turo in Dallas is $40.

III. Toyota C-HR

Results from the analysis above indicate that the average annual earnings for renting a Toyota C-HR in Dallas on Turo are $13,500. Finding the average daily income;

Average daily income=Average Annual Earnings/365

$$=13,500/365=37$$

The Average Daily Earning for renting a Toyota C-HR on Turo in Dallas is $37.

The Average Daily Earnings for the three cars is $125= (48+40+37).

CarSync

Turo has given CarSync to its users, which makes it easier to manage the fleet. The feature is made possible by the Turo app. It is a wireless technology that uses Bluetooth and Voice-activated Navigation to send information between your smartphone and your car. It has given digital mobility business customers the right solutions. It makes it easy to use simple controls like voice commands and buttons on the steering wheel to listen to music or do other things like make and take calls. It lets people connect to information, entertainment, navigation, and different settings. For CarSync to work well, you need a device that can connect through Bluetooth and a media player that can connect through Bluetooth. It is surprising, but the whole fleet can be managed by someone else. It uses IoT and an AI-based management system that learns on its own. This aspect makes it one of the world's most effective systems for managing fleets. Regardless of the number of cars you have listed on Turo, CarSync helps you manage all the reservations and cars in a single place.

Chapter Two: Turo Protection Plans and Vehicle Insurance Covers

Turo Protection Plans

First, you should not confuse insurance plans with Turo protection plans. The two plans are distinct and work in different ways in case of vehicle damage. They also operate under separate legislation. Importantly, they guarantee the vehicle's protection since all fleet owners are always worried about the condition of their cars when transacting with Turo. Additionally, the hosts can choose from five plans that offer reimbursement for repairs. The plan caters for up to the car's actual value in case of damage during a trip. Understanding the difference between insurance covers and Turo protection plans is essential to enhance a beneficial mutual relationship between the fleet owner and the company.

Turo protection plans are not insurance. New Turo hosts refer to the protection plans as "insurance" and think they work like insurance when the vehicle is damaged. The protection plans are not insurance. They are not regulated the way insurance is regulated, and they don't work the way insurance works. The Turo protection plans could best be described as "Responsibility Agreements." Turo is not "double dipping," as some disgruntled hosts contend, who don't understand how this works. With every trip that happens, three separate parties agree to the amount of responsibility they will bear in the event your vehicle is damaged. Here is some more information on the matter:

1. The host chooses a protection plan, and that protection plan determines the amount of the repair cost the host is willing to be responsible for. If you want to be responsible for zero of the repair cost, there is the 60 plan. The full repair cost will be paid to you by Turo, but in exchange, you will earn only 60% of the rental amount for each trip. If you want to earn 90% of the rental amount, there's the 90 plan, but by selecting this "responsibility agreement," you are agreeing to be responsible for up to $2,500 of the repair bill. Then, there are two other levels between the two.

2. The guest chooses (or declines) a protection plan and that "responsibility agreement" determines how much of the repair cost the guest is willing to be personally responsible for. If the guest wants to be accountable for zero of the repair cost, they can choose the Premier Plan, but in exchange for having no responsibility (and putting it all on Turo), they pay the highest fee for this plan. If the guest wants to pay a lower protection plan fee, they can choose the Minimum Plan, pay less, but be responsible for up to $3,000 of the repair cost. There is a Standard Plan between the two, or the guest can decline a protection plan altogether and be held responsible for 100% of the repair cost.

3. The third party, Turo, agrees to be responsible for making sure you are paid the entire repair cost, minus the deductible that you chose with your "responsibility agreement," regardless of what the guest chose or declined. This comes out of Turo's pocket to ensure you are paid back in full.

Even though it is rare for a car to get into an accident during a Turo trip, the guest is expected to inform the host immediately if it does. If you find damage that the guest did not report after the trip, you must tell the claims and resolutions center right away. For reimbursement to be possible under the chosen protection plan, you must follow some steps. The first thing to do is tell the company about the damage within 24 hours of the trip ending. After you report it, a Turo agent will contact you to help you figure out what to do. The next step is to show proof, such as pictures. Take clear photos that show how the car looked at the beginning and end of the trip. Use the app's check-in and check-out features to look at and upload the photos. If you have any concerns or questions, you should talk to a professional in the insurance field for more information.

Deciding on the Most Appropriate Protection Plan

The rules and regulations for Turo protection plans indicate that three parties must agree on the amount of responsibility they will share in case of damage for every trip made on Turo. The Turo protection plan is also described as a responsibility agreement. That is to say, the planning you choose will determine the percentage of cash you will be responsible for in case of damage. In other words, your selected plan determines how much you will have to contribute to catering for the repair cost. For example, you choose the 60 plan, where you will not contribute any cash in case of damage. Turo will fully cater for all the repair costs, but you only earn 60% of the money you earn from each trip you have rented a car on Turo. If you are not satisfied with achieving 60%, then you can go for a 90 plan where you make 90% of the money from each trip. However, the responsibility agreement for this plan indicates that you should be responsible for up to $2500. There are two other levels of crop protection plan between the 60 and the 90 plan.

Another protection plan is the premier plan which allows the guest to pay zero repair costs in case of damage. Turo will be responsible for all the repair costs for this plan, but you will have to pay the highest fee. You can choose the minimum plan if you want to spend a lower protection plan fee. For this plan, you will be responsible for up to

$3000 of the total repair cost. The standard plan is provided between the premier and the minimum plan for guests who decide to take full responsibility for the entire repair cost by declining the protection plans.

Furthermore, you can use Turo, the third-party responsible for ensuring that you earn 100% of the total money earned from each trip minus all the deductibles selected from the protection plan. Turo will ensure they repay all the repair costs from their pockets.

It would help if you chose the plan that best suits the needs of your business. The options include:

- 60 plan
  - Top-tier protection with a full suite of extra benefits.
  - Earn 60% of the cost of the trip.
  - Standard $750,000 in third-party liability insurance.
  - Paid 100% of eligible damage cost by Turo with no deductible.
  - Includes reimbursement of exterior wear and tear.
  - Includes $50 per day replacement vehicle reimbursement or loss of hosting income during a repair.
- 75 Plans
  - Appropriate for solid coverage and minimum deductibles.
  - Earn 75% of the cost of the trip.
  - Standard $750,000 in third-party liability insurance.
  - Paid 100% of eligible damage above the deductibles by Turo.

- ○ $250 deductibles.

- ○ Replacement vehicle reimbursement of $30 per day during repair. The maximum number of repair days is 10.

- ○ Reimbursement on exterior wear and tear is not included.

- ○ Hosting income during repair is not included.

➤ 80 Plans

- ○ With a more moderate deductible, you will pocket more.

- ○ Earn 80% of the cost of the trip.

- ○ Standard $750,000 in third-party liability insurance.

- ○ Paid 100% of eligible damage costs above the deductibles by Turo.

- ○ $750 deductible.

- ○ Vehicle reimbursement during repair is not included.

- ○ Reimbursement on exterior wear and tear is not included.

- ○ Hosting income during repair is not included.

➤ 85 Plans

- ○ Take a larger deductible to earn big.

- ○ Earn 85% of the cost of the trip.

- ○ Standard $750,000 in third-party liability insurance.

- ○ Paid 100% of eligible damage cost above the deductible by Turo.

- ○ $1625 deductible.

- Vehicle reimbursement during repair is not included.

- Reimbursement on exterior wear and tear is not included.

- Hosting income during repair is not included.

➤ 90 Plans

- Highest reward plan for cashing in the highest risk.

- Earn 85% of the cost of the trip.

- Standard $750,000 in third-party liability insurance.

- Paid 100% of eligible damage cost above the deductible by Turo.

- $2,500 deductible.

- Vehicle reimbursement during repair is not included.

- Reimbursement on exterior wear and tear is not included.

- Hosting income during repair is not included.

Understanding Insurance

Insurance has helped many businesses do better in the long run because it pays for any damages or risks that might happen. However, the customer or the insured party must meet certain conditions to get paid for their injury. When you run a rental car business in Texas, the best way to handle insurance claims is to ensure that all your customers know what they need to do to be eligible for insurance after damage. In this situation, the company should work with the customers, their lawyers, and the insurance company to avoid future lawsuits. Customers will always get a Consumer Bill of Rights, which is very important. The government should also get involved in insurance cases for more fairness and openness.

Full Coverage Insurance

This aspect is insurance coverage with liability coverage PLUS comprehensive and collision coverage. Liability coverage, as the name implies, means what you are liable if you get into an accident. So, for example, if you were to hit somebody, the liability portion of your full coverage policy would cover any bodily injury or property damage caused to a third party. Most states have bodily injury and property damage limits required by every driver to carry on their vehicles. A physical damage limit of $100,000 means that the insurance company would only pay $100,000 for each person you injured in a car accident. The second set of numbers, $300,000, is the maximum bodily injury amount they would pay for EVERYBODY that's injured in the accident you caused. Any physical injury medical costs beyond $300,000 will have to be paid by the insured. However, we are not interested in these numbers.

The $100,000 property damage limit is the magic number. This is the most that the insurance company will pay for any damage to any property caused by the insured. This is the only number we are concerned about. The property damage limit determines how much the insurance company will pay for the rental car that the insured is driving. You want the property damage limit to be equal to or more than the value of the car you are giving to the renter. This is very important. Never hand over the keys to a $100,000 BMW to a customer with a $15,000 property damage limit!

Commercial Fleet Insurance

Typically, fleet owners with at least five or more vehicles need to have commercial fleet insurance. To get this kind of policy, you need to reach out to an insurance broker in your area, and they will help you find a commercial insurance policy specific to your state. This aspect is typically relatively easy for vehicles valued at less than $70,000. There are several companies out there, such as G.M.I. and Lula insurance, who will readily take on this type of risk. This trend would be primarily perfect for those running fleets of economy cars or lower to mid-luxury vehicles.

Bonzah.com also offers coverage for specific classes of vehicles up to $35,000. Hybrid insurance models exist where you are only charged once a renter has rented your car, and coverage ceases to exist once the vehicle is returned from the rental. However, the only con would be that these insurance companies do not accept higher-priced vehicles or exotic cars, unfortunately.

Several years ago, many high-end car rental agencies came on the scene in Miami and Vegas. They made a lot of money quickly but also made many bad business decisions and committed insurance fraud to get out of the debt they were overburdened with. Most of them resorted to burning down their fleet or warehouses and filing insurance claims to collect on the money rather than face the consequences of their bad business decisions. They took the easy way out, and unfortunately, the burden fell on the insurance companies to pay out these fraudulent claims. This put a bitter taste in the mouth of insurance providers, and they decided to exit the exotic/higher-end fleet insurance market. Hence, it's complicated to find an insurance company that's willing to underwrite this risk. If you find one, they will typically request a minimum of 10% of each vehicle's Actual Cash Value (A.C.V.) for the insurance premium per year, coupled with a 20% deductible for any claims made. Your average exotic could efficiently run into $20,000-$30,000 per annum per car. These companies will also cancel your policy and blacklist you if you file a claim within the 1st year. Not for the faint of heart. I suggest you reach out again to local brokers in your areas to see if they have any affordable companies willing to underwrite this risk.

Using the Renter's Personal Full Coverage Insurance

Instead of purchasing business fleet insurance plans, most automobile rental companies with vehicles worth $80,000 or more employ this technique. Whole coverage auto insurance policies are required by law to extend coverage to any vehicle the insured may be operating. As a result, as long as I have a policy with full coverage, I can rent any car, anywhere in the world where my insurance provider provides coverage, and my approach will cover the rental. Most car rental companies take advantage of this fact. To take advantage of this, before giving over the keys, you should request the customer's driver's license and proof that they are named as a driver on a valid full-coverage insurance policy. After receiving the full coverage insurance ID card, you should first conduct a Google search for the company's name and phone number. This practice could be a phony insurance card; therefore, do not call the number shown on the card. Google the company's name and customer service number, then phone them to confirm insurance coverage.

What About Non-Owner Insurance?

A non-owner insurance policy will not cover a rental car despite popular opinion. A non-owners policy would only cover the other vehicle that the renter hits. Not your vehicle. Some car rental agencies, out of ignorance, sell this kind of insurance to their renters. It will not cover your vehicle. Do not be fooled by this, nor should you offer this product to your customers.

Selling Secondary Insurance

However, there are some other strategies that we could use. If the renter doesn't have any insurance policy, you could also opt to sell them a secondary renters insurance policy from companies like allianz.com, insuremycar.com, or Sure (by Chubb insurance). These are viable alternatives for providing secondary insurance to your renters. These insurance policies typically cover only up to $70,000, maybe $80,000. No more. This valuation is also based on the M.S.R.P. of the car, not how much you paid for the car when you bought it. This is a very important point. Make sure you know the exact M.S.R.P. value of the car before buying one of these policies. Allianz, for example, would only cover vehicles with an M.S.R.P. of $75,000 or less. Also, you need to be mindful of the effective date of the policies, as insuremycar.com would only start coverage 24 hours after you paid for the policy. So, a policy bought today will not be effective until 24 hours later. This does not do you any good if it's a 1-day rental. If you're willing to purchase in advance, the most viable option, in this case, is insuremycar.com.

How to Manage Commercial Insurance for Private Rental Cars

One way to manage your insurance is to create an LLC. This is a safer way of dealing with your car insurance because this way, your assets are not tied directly to you. Instead, they are tied to the LLC. An LLC is a limited liability company, and it simply works in a way that you are seen as a different entity from the company. Otherwise, if you work as a sole proprietor, all losses and potential problems (being sued, car damages, etc.) that end up costing you a lot of money ends up being directly tied to you. This is why it is smarter to create an LLC – this way, your liability is limited, and you cannot be sued for your assets if you do end up having financial issues. By setting up an LLC, your cars are insured as assets of the *company*, instead of your *own* assets, meaning that you do not need to worry about losing your assets in case the company goes bankrupt or you have problems with your insurance.

To set up an LLC, you will need to check with your state to see the steps to follow. In most cases, you need to sign up for an EIN, declare the members of your LLC, create an individual business name, and prepare the legal forms required to officialize your business. This is discussed in more detail in Chapter 6.

Chapter Three: The Process

Many processes should be followed when starting a rental car business. Below are the key steps:

Step One: The Business Plan

Establishing a proper business plan is the first step toward a successful entrepreneurship journey. A proper business plan requires an effective business strategy. You must also take adequate time to conduct proper market research to ensure you don't use much cash for your rental car agency. A proper business plan may involve building a brand, using a franchise model, or using a car dealership model. In this case, we will focus on owning an independent small business or, in other words, owning a brand. Having a personal or individual business is the best option to take since decisions can be made independently for this model. However, this model requires a lot of time and financial resources. Luckily, I will provide all the necessary information for a successful rental car business in Texas.

For dealerships, you will be expected to set up a legal agreement with a car dealer to provide rental car services to customers. In this case, the customers might be people who have damaged their cars and want to rent a car for a while before theirs is fully repaired. The advantage of this option is that it requires a small amount of time and financial resources. The disadvantage of this option is that the customers will be limited. The last option is a franchise where you acquire adequate support from successful and popular brand names. These companies will receive adequate guidance on starting and growing your business. Companies that provide such services to new entrepreneurs in Texas include J.D. Byrider, Rent-A-Wreck, U-Save Car and Truck Rental, Priceless Rent-A-Car, Sixt Franchise USA LLC, Hertz, and Avis Car Rental.

Step Two: Legality

In this stage, the first thing to do is determine the most preferred business structure. The various business structures include partnership, sole proprietorship, corporation, and limited liability. Establishing a legal entity such as a corporation or a limited liability company is recommended since it protects the business owner from liability for any loss if the business is sued. The owner will be held individually liable for a personal business if the business is sued. However, for a corporation or the L.L.C., the owner and the business are two independent entities. To reduce the fee, you should form the L.L.C. initially and pay the minimal L.L.C. cost. The minimal L.L.C. cost for a business in Texas is $300.

Step Three: Registering for Taxes

Before opening the rental car business, you must register for federal and state taxes. However, you cannot register for these taxes if you have not applied for an E.I.N. The easiest way to apply for an E.I.N. is by fax or mail through the I.R.S. website. Depending on its structure, there are various options for the taxation of the business. For instance, some L.L.C.s benefit from being taxed as an S Corp or corporation. Registered rental car business under sole L.L.C. makes personal and company assets distinct or independent. It is necessary to note that other franchises and state taxes may apply to specific businesses in Texas.

Step Four: Business Bank Account

For effective protection of personal assets, it is recommended for the business owner to use a dedicated banking and credit account for the business, just like we did with our rental car business. It is important to use a separate business account from the personal account to prevent the mixture of personal and business assets in case the business gets sued. Suppose a business is sued, and all the personal and business assists are mixed. In that case, the owner might risk losing all their properties, including personal properties such as homes, cars, and other valuables. Also, having a personal and a separate business account facilitates taxation filing and accounting. Building business credit is also vital for the performance of the business since it helps to acquire credit cards and other sources of finance, with higher lines of credit and better interest rates.

The first step towards building a good credit score is registering your company legally with the state. It is done after identifying your type of business, where the L.L.C. is the most recommended form of ownership in this case since it protects the personal assets from the company assets in case the company gets sued. The second step toward building a good credit score is getting an Employer Identification Number (E.I.N.). It is obtained from the irs.gov website and is absolutely free. You should avoid using other sites to apply for the E.I.N. since they may be costly. The number also acts as the security number or code for your business. The next step is to use the E.I.N. to establish a business checking account. Setting up the business's physical address, phone number, and other contacts is vital for building a good business credit score. You can sign up for a phone service depending on your budget, or you may use free websites if you're not willing to invest in the former. Using your home address or postal code is not allowed when setting up the physical address. As a result, if you do not have a physical address for your business location, you may use free websites to obtain a virtual one. You may also approach local businesses that allow you to use your email address and contacts along with theirs.

Another important thing is getting a Duns number by registering with Duns and Bradstreet. All you need to do is visit their website and sign up. The company will take approximately two weeks to approve your application and define all the information you have provided. After signing up, you should remember that the number you provide is the one the company will use to contact you. Be mindful of the phone number you provided on the website because clients, insurance companies, and other stakeholders will use that number to contact your company. Registering with Net 30 is the next step to allow you to access business credit to be repaid in 30 days. You can only sign up for a Net 30 account if you have a Duns number. Make sure you pay within the first 15 to 20 days to ensure you do not delay with the credit for a good credit score. The final step toward maintaining a good credit score is to sign up with the Nav app, which helps you monitor your business credit score. The credit score will help you identify the loan packages you're eligible for when the time for applying for loans and credits comes.

Step Five: Set Up Business Accounting

All possible sources of income and costs should be written down. They are essential to the business because they help people understand how well it is doing financially. So, accurate and detailed records should be kept to make filing taxes each year easier. With the L.L.C. Expense Cheat Sheet, you can do the same thing.

Step Six: Licensing and Permit

You should obtain the necessary permits and licenses for the business to operate legally in Texas. Failure to do so will lead to hefty fines or even closure of the business. To obtain the permits and licenses in Texas, you need to provide the company's name, apply for the business license and additional statewide license and apply for federal licenses and tax treatment. Texas businesses must collect taxes on sales for the goods or services they provide. If the business operates out of home, a Certificate of Occupancy (C.O.) is required to confirm that the zoning laws, building codes, government regulations, and zoning laws are met. The owner is responsible for obtaining a legal C.O. from the local government if they plan to purchase or lease a location. Therefore, you should review all the zoning requirements and building codes for the business location to ensure that the business qualifies for a C.O.

Step Seven: Business Insurance

Licensing is important for all businesses since it ensures businesses operate lawfully and safely. In other words, a business license protects the business from financial risks and other unprecedented losses. General Liability Insurance is the best type of insurance policy to begin for business. Another preferred insurance policy for a business with employees is the Worker's Compensation Insurance.

Step Eight: Defining the Brand

Companies with the strongest brands stand out in the market, attracting more customers. The brand is what provides the image of the company, as in how the public will perceive the business. The logo is what defines the company's brand. After coming up with the logo, business cards and codes for publication are created. They help to publicize the company by spreading awareness about the company's website. Promoting and marketing the business is another key step that should be considered. However, the cost of publicizing the company and its services must be minimized. The first step towards publishing the business is by using handouts, brochures, flyers, or business cards that exploit the area of expertise and prices of the products and services. They should be placed where the customers can easily reach them. The best trick is to leave them at the entrance or exit of most tech stores. Handing them out to people in social gatherings or events also publicizes the company.

The next step is setting up a website and other social media platforms to reach people online. Joining social groups, clubs, or technology-related organizations will also attract more customers and expose the business. After attracting some customers, the next step is to develop a close relationship with them for high customer retention. It is because the same will enhance word-of-mouth referrals. Effective pricing policies should also be established to avoid overpricing or underpricing.

Step Nine: Creating a Website

With the rise in the use of the internet and modern technology, using a company website to market the services and products is one of the leading marketing strategies today. Although designing and marketing websites was difficult in the past, the current tech tools make it easy for small businesses to design and market their websites. Today it is not even necessary for a person to hire a web developer since the tech tools in place are easy to use. Examples of simple website building tools include Wix, Shopify, Weebly, WordPress, and Squarespace.

Step Ten: Setting Up the Business

After acquiring all the cars and setting up a hosting account on Turo, the next step is to set up the business's physical location. If you want to sell more outside Turo, then it is recommended that you open the physical store in a highly populated area for it to attract more customers. You can increase your income by providing other additional services like repair and car wash services. All services, including deliveries and extras, should be provided in one location for easy accessibility.

Chapter Four: Car Types

Market research indicates that the most rented cars in Texas are Toyota CHR, Chevrolet Corvette, BMW X1, and Chevrolet Tahoe. Diversity in car types and their purposes should be enhanced to attract more diverse customers. The most popular car brands in the market are:

1. Toyota (110)
2. Chevrolet (94)
3. Mercedes-Benz (85)
4. BMW (76)
5. Hyundai (74)
6. Jeep (50)

Statistically, here are the most preferred cars for rent in Dallas.

1. Toyota CHR was introduced in 2017 and has gained popularity in most markets. It is the first choice on Turo since statistics show that it has the highest number of trips compared to others. Surprisingly, they are only three in number on Turo in Dallas, which is a window of opportunity. Evidently, the demand for this type of car is higher than the supply. The low market competition associated with this type of car is an opportunity for a new business.

2. Chevy Cruze economic spectrum. Chevy Cruze is ranked as the highest in demand due to its high number of trips compared to other cars.

3. Chevy Corvette. It is the most performing sports car on Turo. It has the highest daily rates and several trips compared to other sports cars.

4. BMW 5-Series. Although the BMW 3 series has performed well in the market due to its favorable demand and supply, the BMW 5 series seems to be another solid option.

5. Jeep Cherokee. Although it has a shallow daily rate, it has recorded the highest utilization rate. This is despite the high number of wranglers on the website.

6. BMW X-1 has performed extraordinarily well since it recorded an average daily trip of more than 80. The results above are according to the current statistics.

List of Cars and Description

Normal/Economy Cars

1. Tesla Model 3: It is an electric vehicle ideal for rent in Dallas since everyone is eager to have an experience with one. Additionally, its pricing is accessible and has an ideal blend of performance. It is also among the fastest cars, with a speed of up to 358 miles per hour. It is always believed that there is no cheaper way to park a Tesla in your driveway than Tesla Model 3.

The results above indicate that our average annual earnings for Tesla Model 3 are $14676. Finding Average Daily Earnings;

Average Daily Earnings=Average Annual Earnings/365

$$= 14676/365=40$$

The Average Daily Earning for renting a Testa on Turo in Dallas is $40.

2. Chevrolet Spark is a fourth-generation city car manufactured by a Korean company, General Motors (G.M., Korea). Initially, it was marketed with various nameplates and G.M. marques. The third generation Chevrolet Spark was advertised in various markets under its Chevrolet brand, although in some places like New Zealand, it was referred to as the Holden Spark Barina. It has gained popularity globally since it is associated with low purchase and maintenance costs. Thus, it is ideal for renting to low or middle-class customers in Dallas.

The results above indicate that our average annual earnings for Chevrolet Spark are $5939. Finding Average Daily Earnings;

Average Daily Earnings=Average Annual Earnings/365

$$= 5939/365 = 16$$

The Average Daily Earning for renting a Chevrolet Spark on Turo in Dallas is $16.

3. Chevrolet Tahoe is a full-size S.U.V. manufactured by General Motors (G.M.). The 1995 model is a longer 4-door model that has a longer wheelbase. It is appropriate for family vacations or travels since it has adequate seats for a small family and a wide cargo area for language behind the C Pillar. It is appropriate for renting in Dallas since it has been pronounced as one of the most affordable S.U.V.s. It is also a top-ranked best-selling full-size S.U.V. in the U.S.A.

The results above indicate that our average annual earnings for Chevrolet Tahoe are $21, 752. Finding Average Daily Earnings;

Average Daily Earnings=Average Annual Earnings/365

$$= 21752/365 = 60$$

The Average Daily Earning for renting a Chevrolet Tahoe on Turo in Dallas is $60.

Luxury Cars

1. Maserati Ghibli

Maserati Ghibli refers to three types of cars produced by an Italian Automobile company called Maserati. It is appropriate for luxury since it features pop-up headlamps, alloy wheels, and leather front sport seats. The two rear seats are comfy with a cushion without a backrest to make the Maserati Ghibli a 2-door 2 plus 2 fastback coupe. It has a strong engine power with a speed of up to 255 Miles per hour. Renting this car in Dallas will give the business competitive advantage since many businesses on Turo do not rent it in Dallas yet.

2. Range Rover Sport

It is one of the most luxurious cars introduced in 2004 at the North American International Auto Show. In the context of land rover history, it is a sporty, short-wheelbase 3-door coupe and a low-slung. It also has a one-piece skeletal seat and split-folding gullwing doors. Some of its features include a clamshell bonnet and 22-inch alloys. It has a strong engine power with a top speed of up to 180 Miles per hour and a four-wheel drive. It also features a short wheelbase and five doors. It is ideal for renting for luxury, and it has sufficient space even to accommodate a small family. Surprisingly, despite its popularity, many fleets do not rent it in Dallas, making it one of the ideal luxury cars for a new fleet on Turo.

3. Corvette 2021

Corvette 2021 is one of the latest luxury cars that is carving its legacy in the industry. It has more advanced features that make it an idea of luxury purposes. First, its precision makes it one of the unique luxurious cars. The car's unique features include Wireless Phone Projection, Driver Mode Selector Visualization, and FE2 suspension. Its wheel design and balance improve its performance and provide the driver and the passengers with a nice experience. It also has a mid-engine masterpiece that is beautifully sculpted to make it a powerful statement for the car. Most people who have driven this car claim that it is addictive. Its Front Lift and diagonal color touch screen improve its drive. The technologies incorporated in the car, such as color Head-Up Display and Performance Data Recorder, make the car comfy, driving skills, and driving experience. Its components are integrated throughout the car to make it stay in a beautiful and functional form. The machine is also equipped with a thoughtful command center. Since it is one of the unique luxury cars, many fleets have not yet identified its potential, making it an ideal car to introduce to the fleet as a competitive edge.

Other Car Types

1. Mitsubishi mirage

It is among the wide range of cars produced by a Japanese company, Mitsubishi. Despite having a complicated marketing history due to its nameplate, its first four generations have captured a large market in the U.S.A. and other markets such as Canada. It is among the comfortable S.U.V.s ideal for family vacations and travels. It is also associated with low maintenance and purchase cost hence making it ideal for rent to low and middle-class customers.

The results above indicate that our average annual earnings for renting a Mitsubishi Mirage on Turo in Dallas are $10985. Finding Average Daily Earnings;

Average Daily Earnings=Average Annual Earnings/365

$$= 10985/365 = 30$$

The Average Daily Earning for renting a Mitsubishi Mirage on Turo in Dallas is $30.

2. Nissan Versa

Nissan manufactures Nissan Versa in Japan. There are numerous models of Nissan Versa in the U.S. market, but they are most likely similar in size, model, capability, and other features. It is ideal for rent since it serves many purposes due to its interior spaciousness. It also has a configurable cargo alignment.

The results above indicate that our average annual earnings for renting a Nissan Versa on Turo in Dallas are $10202. Finding Average Daily Earnings;

Average Daily Earnings=Average Annual Earnings/365

$$= 10202/365=28$$

The Average Daily Earning for renting a Nissan Versa on Turo in Dallas is $28.

3. Mercedes-Benzes-a-class

It is a popular subcompact car manufactured and marketed by a German company known as Mercedes-Benz. The vehicle was the company's entry-level car. It is long and has a three-door hatchback. It is well known for its strong engine, fast speed, and hardy body. It is also among the luxurious cars since it has a luxurious interior. This explains why it has been nicknamed Baby Benz by most users. The car is ideal for renting in different areas since it can serve many purposes.

The results above indicate that our average annual earnings for renting a Mercedes-Benz-A-Class on Turo in Dallas are $17732. Finding Average Daily Earnings;

Average Daily Earnings=Average Annual Earnings/365

$$= 17732/365=48$$

The Average Daily Earning for renting a Mercedes-Benz-A-Class on Turo in Dallas is $48.

Chapter Five: Registration and Preparing a Rental Contract

After finishing the internal processes and deciding on the most appropriate rental car agency, the next step is to complete the legal paperwork. The legal paperwork involves deciding the type of business entity and registering with the relevant authorities. The business entities can include L.L.C., sole proprietorship, and partnership. The best business entity for rental car business is an L.L.C. or corporation since sole proprietorship will expose the owner's assets to many risks. Any legal action against your business for sole proprietorship will affect the owner's assistance since they are not considered independent entities. For corporations or L.L.C.s, personal assets are distinct from business assets. As a result, any legal action against the business will not affect personal assets such as homes, personal care, or other properties. Contacting an insurance company is necessary to cover the cars and the business's physical location.

A rental contract is a legal contract between the customer and the rental car owner. It covers all liabilities in cars the customer involves in an accident. It provides an accurate explanation of who is responsible for any damage. The rental contract should protect the rights of the customers and the business hence calling for consultation from a legal professional.

Chapter Six: Acquiring Cars

If you can access adequate funds, you can consider buying a new or second-secondhand car. The most important process when purchasing these cars is selecting the most appropriate type of car for the business, depending on the business location. The cost of the cars and the customers served is another factor determining the type of cars purchased. Building a rental car platform is another way of establishing a fleet of cars without owning them. In this case, you act as a connecting point for people who want to hire cars and those who provide cars for hire. Examples of such platforms are Sixt and Zipcar.

When buying our Range Rover 2018, we had to determine the best way to finance the car since it was one of the most expensive cars we've ever purchased. We financed our Land Rover Range Rover Sport 2018 through cash payments since we had saved from the earnings from our fleet on Turo. Cash payment was the most appropriate means of financing the car since it had the lowest interest rate. We bought the car for $62,380, and it records the highest return on investment (R.O.I.). Other ways of financing a car in Texas include:

Dealership: Purchasing a New Car

There are many ways to buy cars in Texas, making it easy. But a business owner needs to choose the best option for their business. Even though everything in Texas is more significant, buying a car is a considerable choice, especially for many. The first thing a company that rents cars needs to do is get in touch with the Texas Department of Motor Vehicles (TxDMV). The main goal of this government group is to make buyers smarter, especially people who buy cars. It helps people who want to buy a vehicle make correct and well-informed decisions. To get a loan for a new car, you must buy it from a dealer. In Texas, all a person needs to buy a new car is a driver's license and proof of insurance. But it is important to remember that a buyer in Texas should not buy a car from a dealership without thinking about important things. Before agreeing to work with the seller, the buyer should research and look for appropriate loan approval and better interest rates elsewhere. For example, credit unions are a better choice than dealerships if you want to buy a car in Texas because they have lower auto loan rates.

The main options for buying a car in Texas are financing and buying from a dealer or someone you might have heard about online. You can also buy a new car from dealerships in Texas. If you have settled on your budget and decided to buy a new car in Texas, you can find a shiny new car at a dealership. However, you should prepare for any add-ons or upselling tactics that can cause the prices of the cars to climb unexpectedly. You should be aware of this at the initial stages of planning to purchase cars in Texas. You should always be firm and confident when making this decision since you will be the only decision-maker during the process at the end of the day. You should be confident when starting the budget and the business needs.

Dealerships have a lot of legal and formal requirements during the process of selling cars. When buying from a dealership, you must have proof of insurance and a driver's license. Texas requires proof of insurance when purchasing from a dealer. The best way to finance is by getting financing through the dealership.

When getting financing through the dealership, you should bring your last two pay stubs, a list of references (though some dealers may not require this), and a bill or something similar that shows your current address and name. You will have to get a loan if you do not have the money upfront to buy a car from a Texas dealer. Even though many dealers offer financing options, you do not have to use a dealer's financing option if you are doing this in Texas. Before agreeing to the dealer's financing, you should research and look for other interest rate options or loan approvals. For example, Credit unions are a better choice than financing through a dealership because they have low-interest rates on auto loans. Before making a final decision, it is best to find and compare your financial options.

Buying a car from a dealership should be clear, transparent, and straightforward. The most amazing thing about buying cars in Texas is that the rules implemented by the state government do not allow car manufacturers to sell cars directly to the customers. However, if you want to buy directly from the manufacturer's showroom, doing so out of state is recommended. Dealerships have acted as an intermediary that protects the customers from skyrocketing or rising prices. It has also given the dealerships full control of whatever car they resell.

Old/Used Car

If you want to buy a used or old car from a dealer in Texas, you will need to take some extra steps. The good news is that the government has established rules, guidelines, and regulations to protect buyers. To buy a used car in Texas, you must have a driver's license and proof that you live there. These rules must be followed no matter who the dealer is in Texas. If you want to finance a used car through a dealership, you need your last two pay stubs, a list of references (some dealers do not require this), and proof that you live in the area. Even if you pay cash for the car, you must provide all the above. You may have to offer financing options like buying a new car from a dealership. I still think it is essential to do your research and look around for the best financing options before making a final decision. Whether you buy a new or used car, you will get a bill for the sale receipt. You will also get an Odometer Mileage Disclosure Form, a

Buyer's Guide, and a signed Certificate of Title. The dealer has 20 days after the sale to change the car's title to the buyer's name.

Fortunately, the Lemon Law in Texas protects the buyers and forces warranties that are still on the vehicle. Although it won't allow you to collect any money on damages, it will force the manufacturer to replace the problem or buy back if the car is still under warranty.

Private sellers

Another option for buying a new or used car in Texas rather than a dealership is buying from private sellers. Although it is the cheapest option, it is associated with many risks. You are always required to make a transfer of the title if, for example, you are not guaranteed a Bill of Sale. When buying a new or used car in Texas, you are expected to have a driver's license, proof of residence, and a pen. That is if you came across a car online. When buying a pre-owned car, the person you are buying from must have a Certificate of Title in their possession. The certificate guarantees that the seller is the current legal owner of the vehicle. You should never walk away from the private sale before obtaining this certificate. The seller can successfully transfer the ownership to you after signing and noting down the odometer's mileage. The title name should be transferred before the end of 30 days from the purchase. Both the seller and the buyer will have to sign the form.

To get curated with the best cars for sale in Texas, you should use apps like the CoPilot car shopping app. You just need to search the type of car you are looking for, and the app will search all the inventories for every dealership to make the best car listings in the area. When buying new cars, you should use CoPilot Compare to search for the listing of new cars on sale. The best way to find early trade-in, off-lease, and C.P.O. cars is to use CoPilot Compare. When using such an app, you should see cars that are no older than five years old. The car should also have low mileage. The good thing about using CoPilot is that it is built with the same technology used by dealers to buy and sell inventories. So, it provides more information about all the cars than other competitors do.

Note: Not knowing how to estimate payments is the worst thing a person can do during a car dealership, a lease, or finance before the salesman gives you a quote. Below is an illustration of how to estimate the payments during a car dealership.

How Can I Finance it?

All this aside, you still need to figure out how to finance your car business. When it comes to purchasing new cars, you have a few options. For example, you can finance it by using the money you have made from the profits of your Turo business. This is a business model that is very common: you save a lot of your initial profits, set them aside, and use them to expand your float later.

You can also finance your cars by taking out small business loans, or specific loans aimed at helping you grow your business. These loans are made for entrepreneurs like you who need a quick source of cash to invest in their business to then expand their business further. To have access to such loans, you will need to provide some information on your cash flow. Investors and/or lenders will want to see that you have the ability to repay it. Therefore, you will need to prove that you have a steady source of cash flow (through your Turo business) as well as a good credit score. For this, you can request to see your credit score to see where you rank. If your credit score is low, you will want to look into credit repair. Once you have a good credit score and cash flow to showcase your ability to pay back any loans you take, you are all set to get started on your financing options.

You also have the option to purchase a car in your business name by using your business account to finance it – this is especially useful when it comes to deducting the cost of the car from your taxes (and hence losing a lot less of your income to taxes that you DON'T have to pay!). Let's get something very important clear: when you purchase a car in your business name, it becomes a business asset, which means that you can write off all the expenses of that asset. There are two ways to do this. Before we go into this in more depth, remember that you should focus on purchasing your vehicle because it then sits as an asset in your accounts. This means that you can also *depreciate* your assets or allocate the cost of your asset and write it off over time, which can take up 7 years (and more if you follow the 6000-pound rule, which is a rule that states that you can deduct a lot more from your car payments if your car is under 6000 pounds). Playing with these deductions is the smart thing to do – it gets you a lot more money in the bank!

There are two ways that you can deduct car expenses. First, you can us the Actual Expense Method, where you quite literally write off all of your car expenses. This includes repairs, oil changes, and trips. You can write up your insurance payments as well as the yearly registration payments. On top of this, you can also deduct the cost of new tires, parking tickets, car washes, windshield wiper fluid, as well as the depreciation of the vehicle, as discussed above.

The next method is the Standard Mileage Method. This is where you can write off all of the mileage of your vehicle. Both of these methods are excellent options when it comes to saving money off of your taxes.

Here are the steps that you should follow to buy a car in your business name.

1. Build your business credit

If you already have business credit, you will not need to worry about providing the car provider with your personal assets as guarantee (i.e., collateral). Therefore, you are not going to be held personally liable if you default on any payments. On the other hand, without this credit, you are risking your personal credit score if anything goes wrong. To do this, incorporate your business (become an LLC). For more on this, have another look at the second chapter where we discussed this in more detail.

2. Decide whether you want to finance or lease the vehicle

Both of these offer the same tax advantages, but depreciation is where things are different. While financing the vehicle, you can deduct the cost of the vehicle throughout its lifetime. If you lease it, you can only deduct it as long as you are leasing it. You should also be careful about the mileage limit – you may need to pay more tax per mile.

3. Purchase car insurance

You need to speak to the commercial sales department of your car dealership. Then, discuss gaining commercial auto insurance.

4. Register the car in the name of your business.

Don't forget to register the car in the name of your business! This is crucial to ensure that you can benefit from all the advantages that having a car in your business name has to offer.

Transferring Private Vehicle Ownership to Business Ownership

The first step involves preparing a title transfer form. To obtain this form, you need to request it from the department of motor vehicles. After obtaining the form, you should contact the insurance agent and discuss the insurance ramifications of transferring the car from private ownership to business ownership. In most cases, the L.L.C. business cost will be higher than private ownership since the insurance companies assume that L.L.C. ownership is associated with more risks and liabilities than private ownership.

It would help if you listed the L.L.C.'s full legal name as the car's new owner. Then, sign the title request after noting that you are the person authorized to sign for the L.L.C. and the private vehicle. The form should be submitted to the D.M.V. as proof of insurance, and it will cater for any fees. You are only required to have a car title and an L.L.C. article of the organization to complete this procedure. The most important thing to note is that moving a private asset to L.L.C. is not advisable to prevent its loss if personal bankruptcy is prohibited.

Chapter Seven: Target Audience

A successful car rental business startup is determined by the ability to target the right customers. Market segmentation is the best business strategy to target the most appropriate audience. Through market segmentation, I have discovered that the most appropriate business audience for rental car business is tourists, car dealerships or mechanic customers, business travelers, and long-term rentals for people who just moved into Texas. It is important to appropriately assess the location and determine the mobility needs of the population. Providing specific services or types of cars that fulfill the customers' needs determines the business's ability to grow. Below is a list of the most preferred target market for a rental car business:

1. Business Travelers

They are individuals who rent cars for business purposes. When attending meetings or work-related events, they hire cars to travel across a new city for a short period. These clients are reimbursed by the company they work for, for the cost of the rented cars. It can be for one or a few weeks. Having such clients is beneficial for a business since they are a reliable source of income. These travelers afford to pay high prices, and they have good credit.

2. Leisure Travelers

These are customers who rent cars for personal use, especially on vacations. They often hire a car for a longer time than business travelers do since they can take trips for weeks or months. They use the car to explore the new place while getting around. They require luxurious, headache-free, and hassle-free cars since they hire cars only when on vacation. As a result, they are ideal for full insurance packages for upselling insurance. The insurance will cover dents or scratches on the rental car.

3. Functional Purposes Renter

They hire cars for functions that last a short period, like a few hours or days. They may require a car for a one-time task such as moving equipment or furniture. They are not concerned with comfort, extras, or luxury but only look for the cheapest car options. As a result, they are ideal for promotions and discounts on prices.

4. Special Occasion Renter

They rent cars for special occasions such as weddings, funerals, dates, parties, and other events or functions. They prefer luxurious vehicles that they won't rent on normal days. It can be a classic sport or exotic car for them to impress others. These customers often pay a high amount just to show off.

5. Large Families with Children

They hire family cars that have five to seven seats. However, suppose the family members cannot comfortably fit in the family car. In that case, they may need a second car for hire to travel together as a family, especially when going for a vacation or trip. The same applies if the family travels with extended family members such as grandchildren, aunties, or uncles.

6. Families without a car

Some families prefer hiring a car if they need one, rather than purchasing and catering for the associated costs. So, whenever they need to travel for a vacation or a trip, they hire a car from a rental car company. They find it more economical since they won't have to worry about costs such as insurance, car payment, fueling, and other associated costs.

Chapter Eight: Digital Presence and Handling Customers

The rise in the use of the internet has forced many businesses to have a digital presence since most customers seek products and services online. Companies ensure digital presence by building apps and websites that help customers access their products and services online. You can hire a professional web developer to build a professional website or app for the rental car business. Social media platforms can also reach many customers and publicize the business. You should also be active online most of the time to build a strong connection with the customers. Responding to texts or comments is part of being active and providing high-quality customer care services. It enhances customer attraction, retention, and satisfaction.

The most effective way of handling customers remotely is by establishing effective remote customer service. To achieve this, the company has to use modern cloud-based project management tools that centralize information in an easily accessible place. It also allows team members to connect and communicate regardless of their location. Another way to remotely handle the customers is by sharing information through a knowledge-based system. Many customers claim that they get satisfactory services when they talk to someone more knowledgeable. The team should also use customer service solutions when solving customer-related problems. For instance, customer services software effectively allows workers to track conversations and monitor customer service relationships when revisiting past conversations.

Chapter Nine: Having Repeat Customers

Although many entrepreneurs face many challenges in attracting new customers when establishing their business, maintaining, or keeping repeat customers has been another challenge for new businesses; luckily, there are several ways of keeping repeat customers. One of the best strategies is selling or supplying the customers with what they need. The key principle to a successful business is that it must solve the customers' needs by providing what they require in the market. Another way to keep repeat customers is to provide high-quality customer care services. The company should ensure that all the needs of the customers are attended to appropriately for the satisfaction of customer needs. Customer personalization and feedback are another way of ensuring they feel engaged with the company and its services (Bleier, Keyser & Verleye, 2018). Furthermore, the company should use promotions and incentives to motivate repeat customers and keep them returning. The same will also ensure that they refer other clients, increasing sales.

Introducing new products such as new car models and other additional services to help retain the customers is essential. This case is since customers like exploring new items and services. It would help if you also emphasized building a strong brand image and marketing it. You can sell the brand using all available technologies such as social media, search engine optimization, Facebook, Instagram, Twitter, TikTok, WhatsApp, and other online platforms. Differentiation will also encourage repeat customers since it gives the company a competitive advantage in the market. Also, following up and getting in touch with the customers will improve customer retention and attraction. The same can be achieved through the phone, email, or the company's website.

Optimize your booking during low season

For most of the country, we're entering the slow season. You're seeing hosts post in the group about how their business has slowed and booking activity isn't what it was over the summer. What do you do to generate maximum bookings during the slow season?

There are three things you should be thinking about:

Seasonal pricing. When you enter the slow season, you are going to need to adjust your daily rates to remain competitive. Every business in the travel, tourism, hospitality, and auto rental industry does this. BUT, be very mindful of your profit margins. Do not engage in a race to the bottom with your pricing.

Self-driven marketing. Now is the time to do some of your own marketing to keep your vehicles moving with locals in need of transportation, when the tourists stop coming. One strategy is to work with your local mechanic and body shops to become their preferred auto rental option for their customers. Put signs up in these places with a QR code to scan directly to your fleet so when people are dropping off their vehicles for repair, they can book one of yours while there.

Settings management. Before you begin dropping your daily rates, make sure your trip preferences are optimized for slow season booking. This should be the FIRST thing you look at before taking any other actions. Here are my recommended trip preferences for slow season.

Turn On Instant Booking

During your peak season, when your cars are booked out without any effort, you should turn off instant booking to select the best guests and most profitable trips. But when slow season begins, you just need bookings, so now is the time to remove that barrier and allow instant booking.

Allow One-Day Trips

During peak season it makes sense to have a 2 or 3 day minimum trip length. When it slows downs, you just need to keep your vehicle moving. Drop your minimum to one day. Many one-day trips will actually become multi-day trips through extensions.

Allow Shorter Weekend Trips

When business is popping, you may require longer weekend bookings. But, when it slows down and you're serving more locals than visitors, again you just need to keep your vehicle on the road so now is the time to relax that requirement.

Allow Short Advance Notice

The longer the advance notice you require, the more bookings you'll miss from people who need a vehicle quickly. During the slow season, shorten this time to the shortest notice you can manage with your schedule.

Keep The Trip Buffer Short

Turo requires a minimum trip buffer of 3 hours between the end of one trip and the start of another. Keep it at three hours. A lot of hosts make the mistake of setting the trip buffer longer, stacked on top of their advance notice, taking the vehicle out of search results for too many hours each day.

Offer Delivery

During peak season you may have enough bookings with people who will pick up at your location that you don't need to offer delivery (In over 2,000 trips I never offered delivery). But, in the slow season, you may need to be more flexible with delivery to keep your vehicles booked. Always charge a high enough delivery fee to make sure that you're not losing money with each delivery.

Order of Operations

Sometimes your booking activity can be significantly improved by simply tweaking your settings without having to cut your rates too deeply. My recommended order of operations during slow season is adjust your settings, then launch marketing efforts, and then adjust rates more aggressively as needed.

Chapter Ten: Marketing Outside Turo, Car Safety, and Maintenance

Marketing Outside Turo

Turo is one of the leading marketplaces that allows private car owners to rent out their vehicles via an online and mobile interface in Texas. Many people own, operate, and earn up to seven-figures with Turo. Nevertheless, entrepreneurs should increase their market sales and performance by seeking markets outside Turo. The rise in internet use and modern technology has made it easy for buyers and sellers to connect online. One of the best ways to market the business outside Turo is through word of mouth, where the business adds its information and URL listing into its email signature. Another traditional way of marketing through word of mouth is asking family members and close friends to spread the word. When using this advertisement, it is important to gather guest testimonials and referrals. In addition, establishing an e-commerce platform for the customers to access the company's products and services online is also an effective way of advertising outside Turo. Advertising online and on social media platforms such as Twitter, Facebook, TikTok, and Instagram is another option for seeking customers outside Turo. Another efficient marketing strategy is localizing the advertisement efforts rather than sourcing customers who might be potential guests traveling from far.

Car Safety and Maintenance

All your cars must have a tracker to avoid complaints of late returns and poor tracking of the car's movement. The price of a good tracker ranges from $30 to $40 on Amazon. It is recommended to get a $40 tracker since it records crucial data like the car's location, how it has been used, and the average speed. It can also tell the current speed at which the vehicle is driven. Always ensure that your car is clean after a trip before handing it over to another client. An Ozone machine helps you achieve this by appropriately washing and vacuuming your vehicle within a few hours. You may not see the essence of buying an ozone machine for ventilated cars, but it is essential to invest in this machine because you may find yourself handing over your vehicle to a client who smokes, and they may return the car with a bad smell. Some clients may do inappropriate things that leave the vehicle smelly. You may not want to hand over the car to another guest in such a scenario, so you need to use an Ozone machine to clean and ventilate the car.

Furthermore, having a spare key and other unlimited forms of unlocking all your cars is recommended. It will save you from situations where a client has lost the key or locked themselves inside the vehicle, and you do not have another spare key. The spare key can also be used with a tracker when the client has delayed with the car and has not provided any communication. In such a case, you only need to use the tracker to identify the location of your vehicle, then you go ahead and unlock it with your spare key and drive it back. Of course, you must report to Turo and communicate with the client through the Turo app. It is also recommended that you warn the client from doing the same in the future to avoid such incidences and inconveniences.

Another critical thing to have as a Turo host is a locker box because it helps you save a lot of time. The average cost for an excellent local box is $50 to $100 on Amazon. The use of a locker box became popular, especially during the Covid-19 period, when guests and hosts used it for self-check-in. You can also request the client to send you a picture of themselves with their ID and the car. The same saves you from situations where a guest hands over the keys to your car to someone else, then they send you a picture of themselves inside the house without the car. A picture of the vehicle, the person, and the ID is another security layer. Composing a list of pre-written texts is another way of saving time. It also improves accuracy and communication with clients through the app. Rather than typing long texts, which may appear sloppy sometimes, you only need to compose a list of pre-written text that you'll be copying and pasting when communicating.

Patience is a virtue for all Turo hosts. People who get in the rental car business come across various clients; some may be good, but some are doing inappropriate things. For example, a client may return your car after smoking inside or doing inappropriate things that make it dirty, but you will not have to charge them a cleaning fee. Reporting them to Turo is also inappropriate since you will not want to have complaints with the company to enhance credibility. This explains why you must invest time and money cleaning your car after every trip. You also need to join an online forum like Facebook groups for hosts where you can get new insights and trends. Such forums will also help you gain more knowledge and skills to help you grow the business.

It is advisable always to ensure that you take your car to a mechanic for a check-up regularly. For a vehicle used for personal use, it is always recommended to take it for service and maintenance once every six months. However, for rental cars, especially on Turo, it is recommended to service them after every 3 to 4 months. You can locate a mechanic near your business location or look for one online. Some websites provide maintenance and repair services to car owners. Yourmechanic.com is an example of a website that has made car servicing, repair, and maintenance easy. All you need to do is to get a quote and book a repair or maintenance service from their website. Their services are provided 24/7. Another thing about the company is that they locate your car and fix it wherever it is, so you do not have to take it to their garage. Their products are also proven high quality because they are long-lasting. It is essential to mention that their prices are fair and transparent. Services provided by the company include car inspection and changing oil and filters. They also replace batteries, timing belts, alternators, spark plugs, starters, fuel pumps, water pumps, radiators, oxygen sensors, thermostats, wheel bearings, and valve cover gaskets.

Chapter Eleven: Successful Rental Car Businesses and Case Studies

There are testimonies of people who started their car rental business on Turo. Some people started with a few cars, but their fleet grew to multimillion-dollar companies with as many as 1,000 vehicles. The testimony teaches entrepreneurs that starting a rental car business on Turo online requires passion, dedication, and effort. These values are vital for a successful entrepreneurship journey. An entrepreneur's narrative is that the initial stages of starting a business are the most challenging phase, but we gain more skills as we grow and advance in the industry. This case explains the need for a mentor who has experienced similar challenges you'll most probably encounter as you manage your business. Below are the testimonies from other successful entrepreneurs on Turo.

Case Study 1: Janik

Through an interview with a successful person who runs Islands rides, Janik (2021) teaches many people who want to start car rental businesses what they need to know (a Turo fleet with 85 different vehicles). He says that he began the fleet with a mini cooper turbo. After making some money with his first car on Turo, he and his wife decided to work together and buy more cars to make even more money. In 2012, they bought a Honda Pilot, and in 2014, they bought a Mercedes G.L.K. Since he did this as his full-time job, the three cars brought in a lot of money. When the number of vehicles went up to

25, he had to hire more people to help deliver them because there were not enough people to do the job. Lucky for him, his daughter finished college, and she and her boyfriend helped support the business. He quickly went from having 20 cars to having 60. After two years, he had saved up enough money to buy enough vehicles, bringing the total to 85. He has sold his old cars and bought new ones. To do this, you must sell vehicles that do not run well and purchase new ones that do. He grew his Turo fleet by increasing the number of cars he had. He also looked at the seasons to determine what kind of car would be best to buy or sell at a particular time of year. He says, for example, that people in his market area (Florida) like sports cars or convertibles in the summer and stronger, fancier vehicles in the winter.

After some time, he could get his place to operate and a dealer's license that enabled him to auction the cars himself. From his statement, it is evident that the best way to sell outside Turo is to obtain a unique place for the business and a dealer's license. With a dealer's license, you can make money from the auction or buy and resell cars directly to clients. Since the cars cannot stay at home, it is necessary to get a parking space for the cars. The company has expanded to R.V. and motorcycle rentals to increase its earnings. The motorcycle rental business earns him approximately $800 per motorcycle every month, which is quite a lucrative deal for him. He has claimed that although Turo is profitable, managing a fleet is tiresome and involves and sometimes not associated with huge profits. Also, your cars can be de-listed from Turo due to minor mistakes such as low tires. He advises the viewers to get an account with AutoZone to repair their cars at an affordable fee. For effective data management, especially after the growth of the business, it is necessary to use an online database or an excel spreadsheet to track the company's operations. He plans to grow his business internationally and increase the number of cars from 85 to 90, then to more than 1000. For trip cars, he provides the customers with all the necessary equipment required for a trip, giving him additional income. For him, it's like killing two birds with one stone.

Case Study 2: Walls

Walls (2022) talks about how he went from being a P2P to running a rental car business. He has spent a lot of time looking for the best way to start a large fleet of rental cars. He went to an I.C.R.S. show, which changed his life completely. He used to run the business of renting vehicles on peer-to-peer platforms like Getaround, HyrerCar, and Turo. Now, he runs a rental car business. He says that he has been managing his fleet with CarSync. As he talks about what he learned and what he did at the show, he talks about how he was able to go to all of the speaker sessions and make connections with many of the present leaders. He learned from other business car owners who were doing well at the same time he was. The show gave him ideas and motivation, making him feel like he could not be stopped. It also made him more goal-oriented in his business.

He tells his audience that even though many people have worked in the rental car business for a long time, no one has ever seen a market like the one we have now. In the current market, anyone can win. In other words, you can either wait for the industry to return to normalcy or be creative or come up with new ways to run the rental car business. Some of the things he learned from other companies that did well include delivering the cars to where the customer lives. An employee is also responsible for picking up the car after the trip. This action was brilliant because there was no need for traditional brick and mortar. So, he tells entrepreneurs to be more creative and develop new ways to do things instead of waiting for the old ways to come back. As an ambassador for I.C.R.S. and A.C.R.A., he promises to guide people and teach them how to market their business outside peer-to-peer platforms like Turo.

Bonus: Summary of the Total Startup Costs

The table above provides the maximum and minimum range of the amount needed to start up a rental car business. With as low as 2461 dollars, you can begin your rental car business either as a retailer or on Turo. However, you can also invest as much as 35923 dollars depending on the depth of your pocket. Generally, the table indicates that flexibility allows one to start a business regardless of the current financial state. The above range seems appropriate for anyone, especially if you do not have such a massive amount of money. The least amount of money provided is more flexible considering the income earned.

Office Fees Expenses

The cost of renting an office space, parking, or car garage is much lower in Dallas compared to other states. From the table analysis, you can start with as low as $0. This is applicable in our case, especially if you are interested in running your business on Turo. If you opt to run your business online on Turo, you will have way more website costs and online advertisement expenses, among other expenses, in the table.

The vacant rate is an economic indicator used by real estate economists and dealers to measure the percentage of vacant spaces for rent or sale. The average cost for renting an office space in Dallas is $30 per square foot. The vacancy rate for these office spaces is 22%.

Employee and Freelance Expenses

In this case, the people who work in an office are the central employees. If you start with a few cars, you may only need to hire one driver for your online rental car business. The driver's only job is to help you bring cars or pick them up from clients. You could also choose to work with just one person as we did with my wife. The number of people who visit a website depends on how good and relevant the content is. This aspect shows why you should talk to an expert or do some research before making a Turo profile. You might find it helpful to remember that on Turo, your brand is based on your profile. Customers think of high-quality services when they see professional profiles. Managing fleets by hand is complicated and time-consuming. The software helps people who own fleets run their businesses more efficiently. Turo is great because it has all the tools you need to manage your fleet well.

Specific Industry Expenses

Renting a car has nothing to do with a specific business cost. Installing a GPS tracking unit is the only technical cost you can have. One GPS tracking unit costs $100 to put in. It should have two or three wires and two antennas to work well. You should not give your car keys to a stranger without first putting a tracker in it. This action is one of the worst things you can do. Even though we trust each other, we should always take precautions to avoid risks we have not seen before. The tracker is essential for this business because it will help you keep track of where your car goes. The fact that there are not many costs for the company shows how easy it is for a person to get into the rental car business.

Advertisement and Marketing Costs

Technological advancement has facilitated marketing and advertising strategies while providing diverse platforms. The leading platforms to advertise the business are Facebook, Twitter, Instagram, YouTube, and LinkedIn. This form of advertisement is referred to as social media advertisement. Other forms of promotion can include TV and radio as they are all primary to creating public awareness about the business. The cost of advertising on Facebook is 7.19 dollars for 1000 impressions, and the price on Instagram is 7.91 dollars. YouTube charges 9.68 dollars per 1000 impressions, and LinkedIn assigns 6.59 dollars per 1000 impressions. Other marketing expenses are incurred when marketing the company's website.

Business Formation Fees

The total cost for business formation is $600. The business will be charged $300 by the Texas Secretary of State as a filing fee plus other state-mandated charges. These fees are applied to an LLC, the most preferred form of business ownership for rental car business (An LLC Registration process is provided in this book).

Website Costs

Hiring a web developer to create your website is approximately $2000. Other charges can be incurred when updating information on the website and paying for hosting. Other ongoing expenses may include monitoring, maintenance, and updating fees.

Vehicle Expenses

It is not compulsory to afford a brand-new car for you to start a rental car business. You can start your fleet with just a single vehicle. You can choose to buy other cars if you want to grow your fleet fast and gain more customers. Some people decide to start a fleet with their car and then save to increase their fleet in the future. In this case, you can either use the vehicle for business and personal ownership or fully transfer the ownership to the business.

Contacts

Email:

btluminarygroup@gmail.com

Instagram

<https://instagram.com/b.t.luminarygroup?igshid=YmMyMTA2M2Y=>>

Check out this awesome host, Louise B., on Turo and grab the keys to your next adventure.

https://turo.com/drivers/18114757

3 TikTok

www.tiktok.com/@joewill105

Facebook

https://www.facebook.com/BTLUMINARYGROUP

Our Turo Profile and Customers Reviews

Louise Bissek is Tchango's fiancée, and they are working together on turo. The pair decided to work together on a common goal: launching their rental car business. This is their Turo profile.

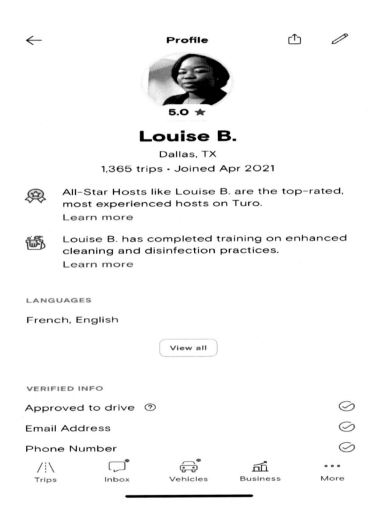

7:38   ·ıll 🛜 20

Business

EARNINGS   PERFORMANCE   **REVIEWS**

★★★★★
Samantha B. Dec 14, 2022
BMW X1 2017

So thankful for Louise for accepting my reservation and delivering my vehicle within three hours. My original host cancelled two hours before I was scheduled to pick up the car. I don't care how far away they are from me, I'll be renting from their fleet again.

Leave a public response

★★★★★
Henry G. Dec 14, 2022
Toyota Corolla 2020

★★★★★
Tim G. Dec 13, 2022
Volkswagen Atlas 2018

★★★★★
Frederick C. Dec 13, 2022
BMW X1 2017

★★★★★
Evelyn W. Dec 13, 2022
Volkswagen Tiguan 2020

All vehicles ⌄   Last 365 days ⌄

Trips   Inbox   Vehicles   Business   More

7:39   ·ıll 🛜 20

Business

EARNINGS   PERFORMANCE   **REVIEWS**

Nissan Sentra 2021

★★★★★
Yesenia W. Nov 22, 2022
Mazda CX-5 2021

Had to rent a car last minute due to the airport rental company being overbooked. Car was ready to go in 2 hours, super clean and nice! So convenient and had the option to drop it off at the airport.

Leave a public response

★★★★★
Hailey B. Nov 22, 2022
Volkswagen Tiguan 2020

Louise was an excellent host. The car was immaculate, she was prompt and had the car right outside of luggage claim for us. Louise was super communicative and made everything so easy.

Leave a public response

★★★★★
Erin C. Nov 22, 2022
Volkswagen Atlas 2018

★★★★★

All vehicles ⌄   Last 365 days ⌄

Trips   Inbox   Vehicles   Business   More

7:38 .ıl 🛜 20

Business

EARNINGS   PERFORMANCE   **REVIEWS**

★★★★★
Victor B. Dec 5, 2022

Hyundai Accent 2021

Host: Prompt communicator, easy to work with and professional. Car: Clean, non-damaged and in perfect mechanical condition very reliable. I would definitely be happy to do business with again in the future. Overall, a great experience.

Leave a public response

★★★★★
Lakindra W. Dec 5, 2022

Volkswagen Jetta 2018

This was my first time using Turo and Louise made the process very easy and very professional. The car was very clean and the rode smoothly and great on gas, I would recommend and use Louise services again.

Leave a public response

★★★★★
MYRA P. Dec 5, 2022

Jeep Cherokee 2020

Excellent experience! rental was easy and veh was clean, delivered on time. Louise was a great host, flexible and very responsive to changes.

All vehicles ⌄   Last 365 days ⌄

Trips   Inbox   Vehicles   Business   More

7:39 .ıl 🛜 20

Business

EARNINGS   PERFORMANCE   **REVIEWS**

★★★★★
Vinesh P. Nov 6, 2022

Volkswagen Atlas 2018

We book this car a few hours before and Louise was great in preparing the car for us in a short time. We loved the space and how it accommodated a family of 8. Louise was extremely helpful in the logistics of dropping the car to us and the return part was so smooth. It was our 1st time using Turo and can't believe how easy and straightforward it was and I can't thank Louise enough for making our trip very pleasant.

★★★★★
Ericka J. Nov 6, 2022

Volkswagen Jetta 2018

★★★★★
Colin G. Nov 6, 2022

Toyota C-HR 2018

★★★★☆
Brittany R. Nov 5, 2022

Volkswagen Atlas 2018

★★★★★
Carey P. Nov 5, 2022

All vehicles ⌄   Last 365 days ⌄

Trips   Inbox   Vehicles   Business   More

71

7:39   .ıll 🛜 20

Business

EARNINGS   PERFORMANCE   **REVIEWS**

Leave a public response

Nardos M. Nov 14, 2022

Toyota Corolla 2020

A booking I made canceled on me last minute as I was on the way to the airport. I booked with Louise last minute and it couldn't have gone any smoother or more pleasant as it did! Car was at the Airport ready for me once I landed and the car is a great ride! Thank you Louise, I appreciate it!!

 ★★★★★

Mark S. Nov 13, 2022

Chevrolet Tahoe 2016

★★★★★

Eric R. Nov 13, 2022

Hyundai Santa Fe 2019

We had a few hiccups- nothing that was anyone's fault, but Louise was cool and calm and handled everything so quickly and efficiently. We would rent from her again in a heartbeat. Car was great, trip was great and having peace of mind was great.

Tyler H. Nov 13, 2022

All vehicles ∨   Last 365 days ∨

⫽\   🗇   🚘   📊   •••
Trips   Inbox   Vehicles   Business   More

7:40   .ıll 🛜 20

Business

EARNINGS   PERFORMANCE   **REVIEWS**

Kyle J. Oct 31, 2022

Land Rover Range Rover Sport 2018

This vehicle was very nice and clean like the picture depicted. No issues at all. Easy pick up and easy drop off. No complaints and would definitely use this person again.

 ★★★★★

Sherenta W. Oct 30, 2022

Hyundai Accent 2021

 ★★★★★

Charlie A. Oct 30, 2022

Toyota Corolla 2020

Lousie was a great host & very accommodating! Will definitely rent from her again!

 ★★★★★

Soreti T. Oct 29, 2022

Nissan Sentra 2017

She's so nice, I highly recommend 10/10

★★★★★

Robert D. Oct 29, 2022

Mazda CX-5 2021

First, Louise was a delight to work with, she was efficient and very personable. Thank you

All vehicles ∨   Last 365 days ∨

⫽\   🗇   🚘   📊   •••
Trips   Inbox   Vehicles   Business   More

References

Alghamdi, A. A. (2020). Feasibility of CAV Delivery Service in Rural Areas (Doctoral dissertation, the University of Hawai'i at Manoa).

Aubrey Janik (2020). Inside the $100,000 PER MONTH Turo Fleet (85 Cars!). Retrieved from: https://youtu.be/nYSD2L6_XdI

Bleier, A., Keyser, A. D., & Verleye, K. (2018). Customer engagement through personalization and customization. In Customer engagement marketing (pp. 75-94).

 Lopez, M. (2019). Texas Insurance Companies—Good Faith Litigant or Litigation Chess Master? A Call to Action for the Texas Legislature. A Call to Action for the Texas Legislature (February 1, 2019).

Palgrave Macmillan, Cham. Chin, K., Gold, A., Bruce, M., Werner, M., Moore, M., Maples, H., & Walton, C.M. (2021). Technology Utilization Plan [for the Texas Technology Task Force] (No. FHWA/TX-20/0-6999- 21-R1). Texas. Department of Transportation. Research and Technology Transfer Office.

Made in the USA
Las Vegas, NV
24 November 2024